LIGHTNING
BOLT
BOOKS™

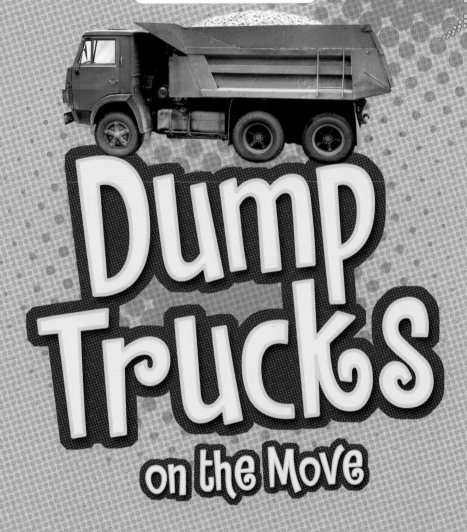

Dump Trucks
on the Move

Judith Jango-Cohen

Lerner Publications
Minneapolis

Dedicated to
Mrs. Ski, with
loads of thanks
—J.J.C.

Lerner Publications Company
A division of Lerner Publishing Group, Inc.
241 First Avenue North
Minneapolis, MN 55401 USA

For reading levels and more information, look up this title at www.lernerbooks.com.

Library of Congress Cataloging-in-Publication Data

Dump trucks on the move / by Judith Jango-Cohen.
      p.   cm. — (Lightning bolt books™ — Vroom-vroom)
   Includes index.
   ISBN 978–0–7613–3917–5 (lib. bdg. : alk. paper)
   ISBN 978–0–7613–7228–8 (eb pdf)
   1. Earthwork—Juvenile literature. 2. Dump trucks—Juvenile literature. I. Title.
   TA732.J3523 2011
   629.225—dc22   2009043794

Manufactured in the United States of America
3–45160–10059–12/1/2017

Contents

Mountain Movers — page 4

Fill and Dump — page 10

Dump Truck Jobs — page 16

Giant Machines — page 20

Dump Truck Diagram — page 28

Fun Facts — page 29

Glossary — page 30

Further Reading — page 31

Index — page 32

Mountain Movers

How do you move
a mountain?

Get a dump truck!

This dump truck
has a full load!

Dump trucks carry big loads from place to place. Then they dump the loads.

Dirt pours out of the back of this dump truck.

This truck is moving
a load of snow.

The snowy load goes into the bed.

The driver rides inside the cab.
Does the driver ever get into the bed?

This dump truck driver sits up high in the cab of her truck.

This driver gets into the bed to cover his load. The cover keeps the snow from falling off onto the road.

The driver pushes these levers
to make his truck dump.

What do the levers do?

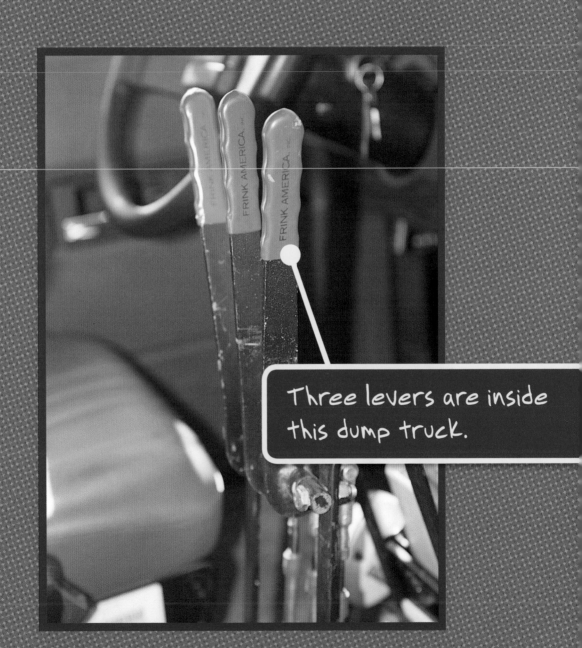

Three levers are inside
this dump truck.

Fill and Dump

Levers make a piston slide out. The piston tips back the bed. The back of the truck opens up.

A piston near the cab pushes up one end of the truck's bed.

WHOOSH! Out slips the snow.
This is how dump trucks dump.
But how are they filled?

A dump truck
full of snow
empties its load.

A front-end loader can fill a dump truck. This loader picks up broken branches.

The front-end loader lifts the branches. They crack and crash into the dump truck's bed.

This front-end loader packs branches into the dump truck.

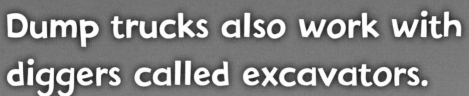

Dump trucks also work with diggers called excavators. Excavators dig holes with their spiky buckets.

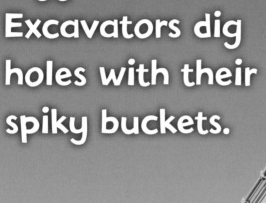

The spikes on the edge of this excavator's bucket help it grab big scoopfuls of dirt.

The spikes rip into the dirt.
CLUNK! CLANG! BANG!
Dirt and rocks drop into the
truck.

Dump Truck Jobs

Dump trucks move branches and snow. They move dirt dug from holes. But some dump trucks help fill holes.

This dump truck prepares to haul away a load of dirt.

A full dump truck roars down the highway.

This truck is loaded with asphalt. Asphalt fills holes in roads.

Do you know what the doors are for?

The driver opens the doors to let hot asphalt pour out.

A dump truck driver fills a hole with asphalt.

Then the driver presses the hot asphalt into the hole.

Giant Machines

Some dump trucks never travel on roads. They are too big.

This dump truck works at a pit where people dig up rock. The truck is so big that a ladder leads up to the cab.

A ladder allows the driver of this large dump truck to climb into the cab.

The wheels of this truck are bigger than the driver.

This truck's wheels are gigantic!

The dump truck carries a load of big rocks. It rumbles up a dusty path.

Rocks fill the bed of this huge dump truck.

The driver stops at the top of the path. He tips back the bed.

This driver looks behind him as he backs up.

The load of big rocks drops
into the crusher.
The crusher will
crunch the rocks into
smaller stones.

Now a mountain of crushed stone must be moved to people who are making a road.

Crushed rock piles up. It's ready for a ride to the construction site!

What luck!

Here comes a dump truck.

Dump Truck Diagram

cover

bed

load

cab

piston

wheel

Fun Facts

- Dump trucks sometimes work at mines. They carry rocks filled with bits of gold, silver, and diamonds.

- If a dump truck is too big to be driven to a work site on roads, it is brought there in pieces. Workers put the truck together at the work site.

- Some dump trucks have lights that flash when the bed is almost full.

- One tire on a giant dump truck may weigh more than three cars.

- Some dump trucks have eighteen wheels.

Glossary

asphalt: a black, sticky material used to make roads

bed: the back part of a dump truck where things are carried

crusher: a machine that breaks big rocks

excavator: a large machine that digs holes

front-end loader: a machine with a shovel in front that scoops and pours

lever: a control that a driver pushes to make a dump truck dump

load: the things that dump trucks carry

piston: a metal rod that pushes up the back of a dump truck so it can dump

Further Reading

Brecke, Nicole, and Patricia M. Stockland.
Cars, Trucks, and Motorcycles You Can Draw.
Minneapolis: Millbrook Press, 2010.

Caterpillar. *C Is for Construction: Big Trucks and Diggers from A to Z.* San Francisco: Chronicle Books, 2003.

Enchanted Learning: Vehicle Online Coloring Pages
http://www.enchantedlearning.com/vehicles/
paintonline.shtml

Lyon, George Ella. *Trucks Roll!* New York: Atheneum Books for Young Readers, 2007.

Morganelli, Adrianna.
Trucks: Pickups to Big Rigs. New York: Crabtree, 2007.

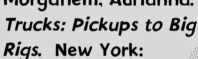

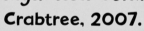

Index

asphalt, 17–19

bed, 6–8, 10, 13, 24, 28–29

driver, 7–9, 18–19, 22, 24
dumping, 5, 9–11, 18, 25

load, 5–6, 8, 23, 25, 28
loading, 13, 15

moving, 4, 6, 16, 26

size, 20–22, 29

wheels, 22, 28–29

Photo Acknowledgments

The images in this book are used with the permission of: © Kuzma/Dreamstime.com, p. 1; © iStockphoto.com/Nancy Brammer, p. 2; © Norman Bateman/Dreamstime.com, p. 4; © H. Mark Weidman Photography/Alamy, p. 5; AP Photo/The Canadian Press, Jonathan Hayward, p. 6; © DANIEL LECLAIR/Reuters/CORBIS, p. 7; © Judith Jango-Cohen, pp. 8, 9, 12, 13, 25; © iStockphoto.com/sumbul , p. 10; © Stephen Morriss/Alamy, p. 11; © Wormseed/Dreamstime.com, p. 14; © IndexStock/SuperStock, p. 15; © iStockphoto.com/Julio de la Higuera Rodrigo, p. 16; © Robert Pernell/Dreamstime.com, p. 17; © Peter Glass/Alamy, p. 18; © Maigi/Dreamstime.com, p. 19; © Per-Anders Pettersson/Reportage/Getty Images, p. 20; © Transtock/SuperStock, p. 21; © Flirt/SuperStock, p. 22; © Bill Bachman/Alamy, p. 23; © age fotostock/SuperStock, p. 24; © Mikhail Olykainen/Dreamstime.com, p. 26; © iStockphoto.com/Mike Clarke , p. 27; © Laura Westlund/Independent Picture Service, p. 28; © Gualberto Becerra/Dreamstime.com, p. 30; © iStockphoto.com/Andre Comeau , p. 31.

Cover: © Inna Felker/Dreamstime.com (top); © James Colin/Dreamstime.com (bottom).